PIANO / VOCAL / GUITAR

THE AMERICANA SONGBOOK

ISBN 978-1-5400-2656-9

Visit Hal Leonard Online at
www.halleonard.com

Contact Us:
Hal Leonard
7777 West Bluemound Road
Milwaukee, WI 53213
Email: info@halleonard.com

In Europe contact:
Hal Leonard Europe Limited
42 Wigmore Street
Marylebone, London, W1U 2RN
Email: info@halleonardeurope.com

In Australia contact:
Hal Leonard Australia Pty. Ltd.
4 Lentara Court
Cheltenham, Victoria, 3192 Australia
Email: info@halleonard.com.au

ALABAMA PINES

Words and Music by
JASON ISBELL

ANGELS FROM MONTGOMERY

Words and Music by
JOHN PRINE

D.S. al Coda

those years just flow by like a bro-ken-down dam.

CODA

hard way to go.

There's flies in the kitch-en, I can hear 'em there buzz-in',

BARTON HOLLOW

Words and Music by JOHN PAUL WHITE
and JOY WILLIAMS

Ooh, _____ ooh, ___ ooh, _____ ooh. ___

I'm a dead man ___ walk-ing ___ here. ___ That's the least of ___ all my ___ fears. ___ Ooh, _____ un-der-neath ___

Won't do me no good wash-ing in the riv- er. Can't no preach-er man save my

soul. Oh, oh,

oh. Did that full moon force my hand?

Or that un - marked hun - dred grand? Ooh,

BIRMINGHAM

Words and Music by CARY ANN HEARST
and MICHAEL TRENT ROBINSON

Moderate Bluegrass feel, in 2

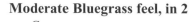

Del - ta Ma - ma and a Nick - a - jack Man   raised their

Cum - ber - land daugh - ter in a Ten - nes - see band,

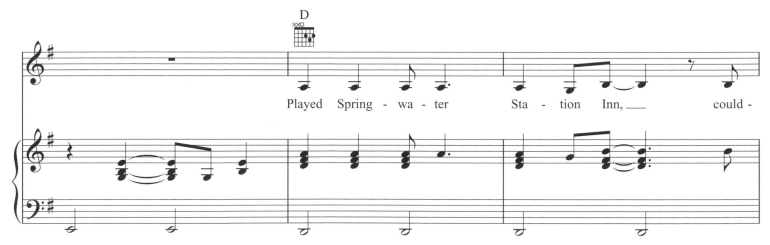

Played Spring - wa - ter Sta - tion Inn, ___ could-

five hun - dred miles _____ from Bir -

- ming - ham. _____

Well, Rock - a - mount Cow - boy in a rock and roll band plugged his

am - pli - fi - er in all a - cross _____ the land.

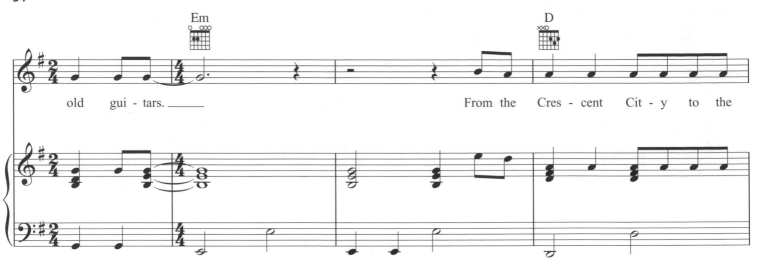

old gui - tars. _____ From the Cres - cent Cit - y to the

Great Salt Lake, it ain't ___ what you got, it's - a what you make.

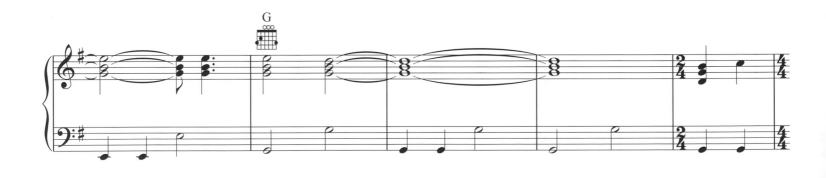

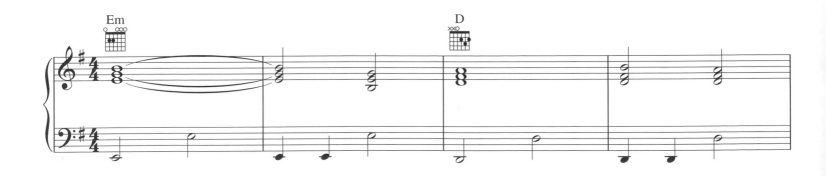

CHOCTAW BINGO

Words and Music by
JAMES McMURTRY

Moderately, in 2

1. Strap ___ them kids in, give 'em a lit - tle bit of vod - ka in a

cher - ry Coke. We're goin' to O - kla - ho - ma to the

com-in' down from Kan - sas and from West Ar - kan - sas. It -'ll be one

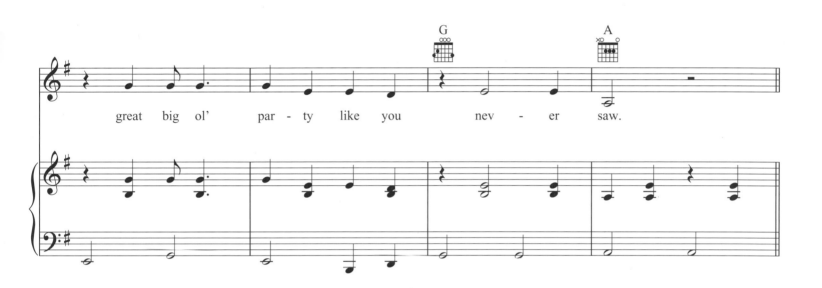

great big ol' par - ty like you nev - er saw.

Piano solo - ad lib.

2. Un - cle Sla - ton's got his Tex - an pride,
3.–7. *(See additional lyrics)*

back in the thick - ets with his ____ A - sian bride. He's got an

Air - stream trail - er and a Hol - stein cow.

He still ____ makes whis - key 'cause he still ____ knows how. He plays that

Additional Lyrics

3. My cousin Roscoe, Slaton's oldest boy
   From his second marriage up in Illinois,
   He's raised in East St Louis by his mama's people,
   Where they do things different. Thought he'd just come on down.
   He's goin' to Dallas, Texas in a semi truck
   Caught from that big McDonald's, you know, the one that's built up on that
   Great big ol' bridge across the Will Rogers Turnpike.
   Took the Big Cabin exit, stopped and bought a carton of cigarettes
   At that Indian smoke shop with the big, neon smoke rings
   In the Cherokee nation. Hit Muskogee late that night.
   Somebody ran the stoplight at the Shawnee bypass.
   Roscoe tried to miss him, but he didn't quite.
   (Instrumental)

4. Bob and Mae come up from some little town
   Way down by Lake Texoma where he coaches football.
   They were 2-A champions now for two years running,
   But he says they won't be this year, no, they won't be this year.
   And he stopped off in Tushka at that pop knife and gun place.
   Bought a SKS rifle and a couple full cases of that
   Steel core ammo with the berdan primers
   From some East Bloc nation that no longer needs 'em.
   And a Desert Eagle; that's one great big ol' pistol.
   I mean, fifty caliber made by bad-ass Hebrews.
   And some surplus tracers for that old BAR of Slaton's.
   As soon as it gets dark, we're gonna have us a time.
   We're gonna have us a time.
   (Instrumental)

5. Ruth Ann and Lynn come down from Baxter Springs.
   That's one hell-raisin' town way down in southeastern Kansas.
   Got a biker bar next to the lingerie store
   That's got Rolling Stones lips up there in bright pink neon,
   And they're right downtown where everyone can see 'em,
   And they burn all night, you know, they burn all night.
   You know, they burn all night.
   (Instrumental)

6. Ruth Ann and Lynn, they wear them cut-off britches
   And those skinny little halters, and they're second cousins to me.
   Man, I don't care; wanna get between 'em
   With a great big ol' hard-on like a old bois d'arc fence post
   You could hang a pipe rail gate from, do some sister twisters
   'Til the cows come home and we'd be havin' us a time.
   (Instrumental)

7. Uncle Slaton's got his Texan pride
   Back in the thickets with his Asian bride.
   He's cut that corner pasture into acre lots.
   He sells them owner financed strictly to them
   That's got no kind of credit 'cause he knows they're slackers
   And they'll miss that payment. Then he takes it back.
   He plays that Choctaw Bingo every Friday night.
   He drinks his Johnny Walker at that club 69.
   We're gonna strap those kids in, give em' a little bit of Benadryl
   In a cherry Coke. We're goin' to Oklahoma, gonna have us a time.
   We're gonna have us a time.

BROKEN HALOS

Words and Music by CHRIS STAPLETON
and MIKE HENDERSON

CAR WHEELS ON A GRAVEL ROAD

Words and Music by
LUCINDA WILLIAMS

Moderate Country feel

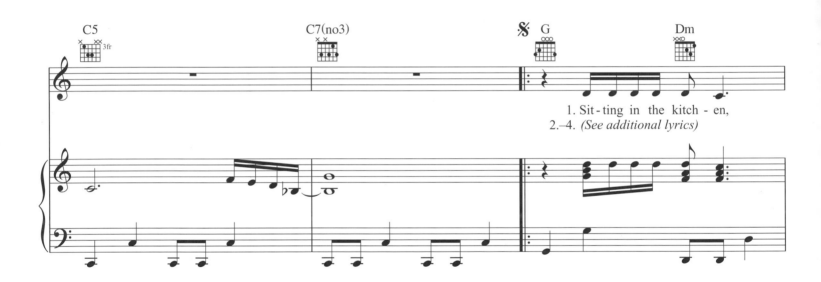

1. Sit-ting in the kitch-en,
2.–4. *(See additional lyrics)*

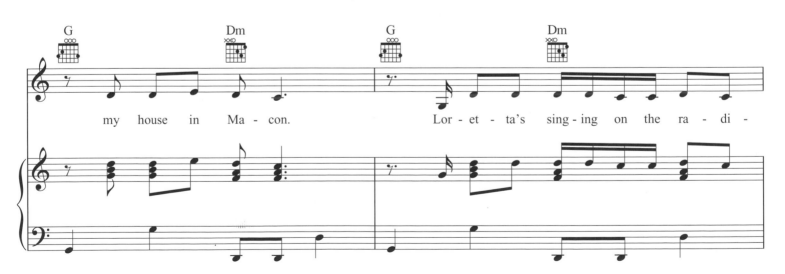

my house in Ma-con. Lor-et-ta's sing-ing on the ra-di-

* *Recorded a half step lower.*

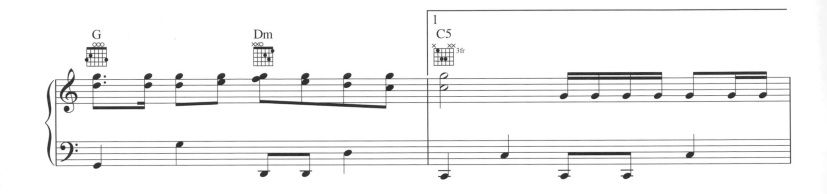

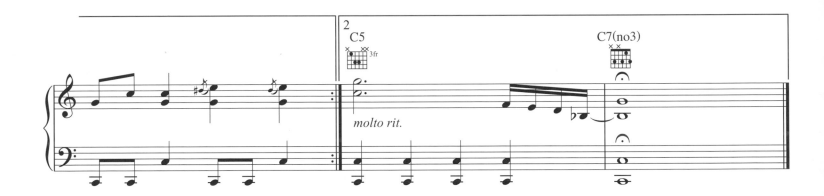

Additional Lyrics

2. Can't find a damn thing in this place;
   Nothing's where I left it before.
   Set of keys and a dusty suitcase.
   Car wheels on a gravel road.
   There goes the screen door slamming shut.
   You better do what you're told.
   When I get back, this room better be picked up.
   Car wheels on a gravel road.
   Car wheels on a gravel road.
   Car wheels on a gravel road.

3. Low hum of voices in the front seat,
   Stories nobody knows.
   Got folks in Jackson we're going to meet.
   Car wheels on a gravel road.
   Cotton fields stretching miles and miles,
   Hank's voice on the radio.
   Telephone poles, trees and wires fly on by.
   Car wheels on a gravel road.
   Car wheels on a gravel road.
   Car wheels on a gravel road.

4. Broken-down shacks, engine parts.
   Could tell a lie, but my heart would know.
   Listen to the dogs barking in the yard.
   Car wheels on a gravel road.
   Child in the backseat, 'bout four or five years,
   Looking out the window.
   Little bit of dirt mixed with tears.
   Car wheels on a gravel road.
   Car wheels on a gravel road.
   Car wheels on a gravel road. *(To Coda)*

A FEATHER'S NOT A BIRD

Words and Music by ROSANNE CASH
and JOHN LEVENTHAL

I'm go- in' down to Flo-rence, gon- na wear a pret- ty dress.
nev- er an- y high-way when you're look- in' for the past.

I'll sit a- top the mag- ic wall with the
The land be- comes a mem-'ry and it

voic- es in my head. Then we'll
hap- pens way too fast. The

Vocal line written one octave higher than sung.

drive on through to Mem-phis, past ____ the strong-est shoals.
mon-ey's all in Nash-ville, but the lights in - side my head.

Then on to Ar-kan-sas just to touch the gum-bo soul.
So, I'm go - in' down to Flo-rence just to learn to love the thread.

Cm/E♭

A feath-er's not a bird, the

Fm7   A♭   B♭

rain is not the sea, a stone is not a moun-tain, but a riv - er runs

COPPERHEAD ROAD

Words and Music by
STEVE EARLE

Moderately, in 2

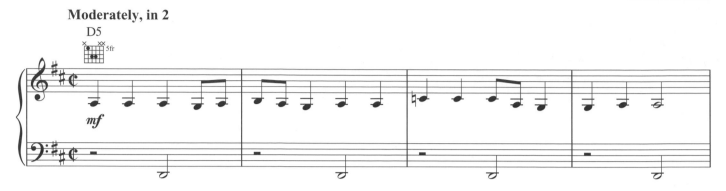

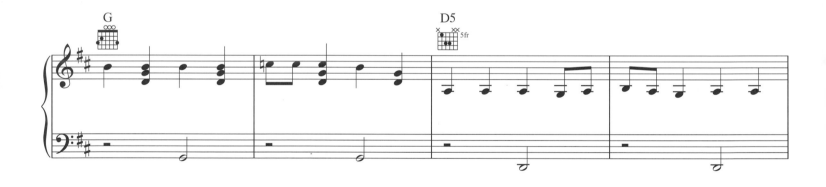

Well, my name's John Lee Pet-ti-more.

Same as my dad-dy and his dad-dy be - fore.

You hard-ly ev - er saw Gran - dad-dy down here.

He on - ly come to town a - bout twice a year.

He'd buy a hun-dred pounds of yeast and some cop-per line.

Now Dad-dy ran whis-key in a big black Dodge.

He bought it at an auc-tion at the Ma-son's Lodge.

John-son Coun-ty Sher-iff paint-ed on the side,

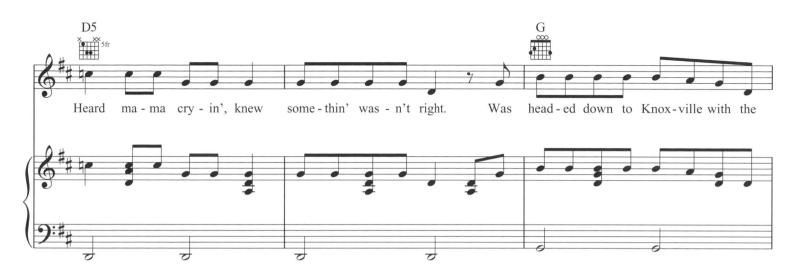

Heard ma-ma cry-in', knew some-thin' was-n't right. Was head-ed down to Knox-ville with the

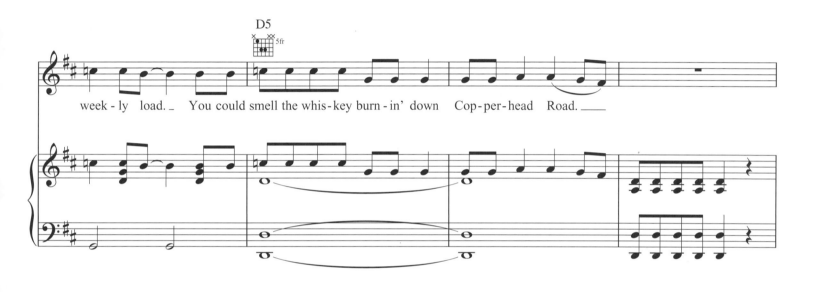

week-ly load. __ You could smell the whis-key burn-in' down Cop-per-head Road. ____

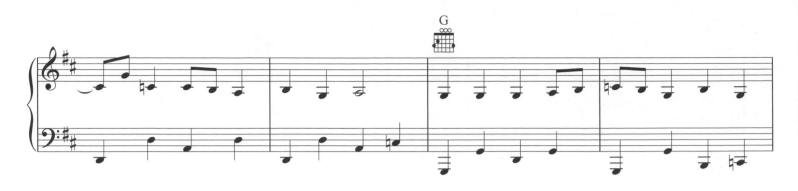

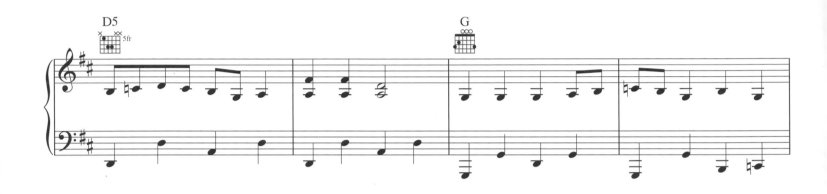

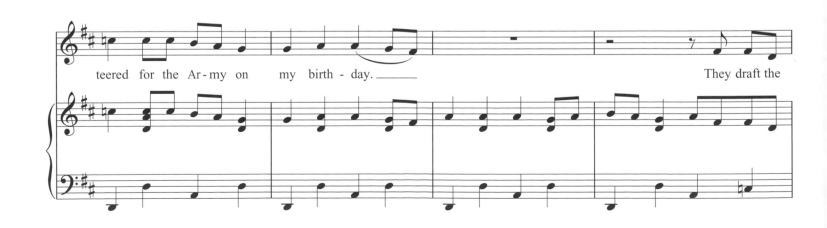

teered for the Ar-my on my birth-day. _____ They draft the

THE EYE

Words and Music by TIM HANSEROTH
and BRANDI CARLILE

It real-ly breaks my heart ___
Where did you learn to walk? ___

to see a dear old friend
Where did you learn to run

* *Recorded a half step lower.*

on - ly if ____ you're stand - ing in ____ the eye. ____

I am a stur - dy soul, _____

GUITAR TOWN

Words and Music by
STEVE EARLE

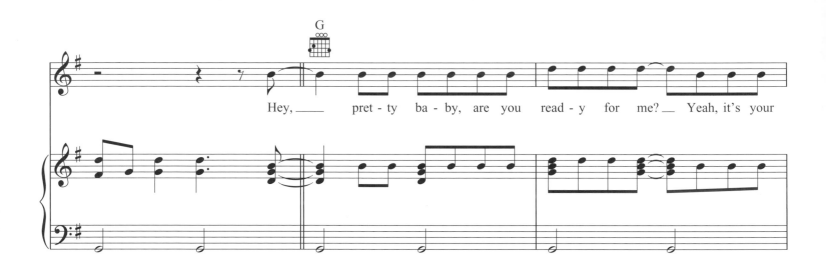

Hey, ___ pret-ty ba-by, are you read-y for me? ___ Yeah, it's your

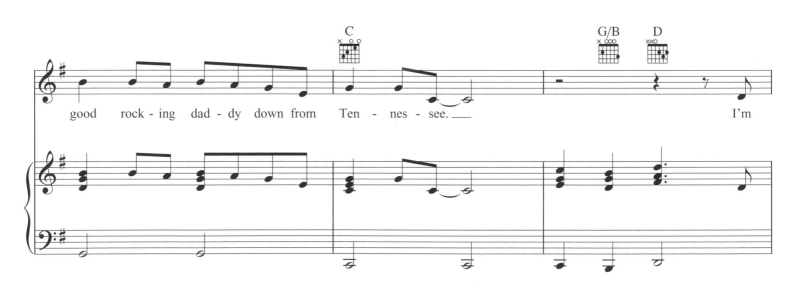

good rock-ing dad-dy down from Ten-nes-see. ___ I'm

just out of Aus - tin, bound for San An - ton', __ with the ra - di - o blast - ing and the

bird dog on. There's a

speed trap up a - head in Sel - ma Town, __ but no lo - cal yo - kel's gon - na

shut me down. __ 'Cause me and my boys __ got this

rig un - wound, __ and we've come a thou - sand miles from a gui - tar

town.

Noth - ing ev - er hap - pened 'round my __

Now I'm smok-ing in-to Tex-as with the ham-mer down,__ and a

rock-ing lit-tle com-bo from the gui-tar town.

One of these days I'm gon-na set-tle down, _ and

take you back with me to the gui-tar town.

(Vocal 1st time only)

HARLEM RIVER BLUES

Words and Music by
JUSTIN TOWNES EARLE

Lord, I'm go - ing up - town to the Har - lem Riv - er to ____ drown. Dirt - y wa - ter gon - na cov - er me o - ver and I'm ____

Har - lem Riv - er to ____ drown.   Dir - ty wa - ter gon - na

cov - er me o - ver and I'm ____ not gon - na make ____ a sound.

Lord, I'm go - ing up -

town to the Har - lem Riv - er to ___ drown.

HELLO IN THERE

Words and Music by
JOHN PRINE

Old peo - ple just grow lone -

- some, wait - ing ___ for some - one to say, "Hel -

lo in there, _____ hel - lo."

So, if you're walk - ing down the street ___ some - time

HELPLESSNESS BLUES

Words and Music by
ROBIN PECKNOLD

I'd work 'til I'm _____ raw; _____ _____ if I _____ had an or - chard I'd work 'til I'm ___ sore. And you ___ could wait

if I _____ had an or - chard I'd
oh, _____ oh, oh, _____ oh,

work 'til I'm ___ sore;
oh, _____ oh.

if I _____ had an or - chard I'd work 'til I'm ___

sore. Oh,

IF I HAD A BOAT

Words and Music by
LYLE LOVETT

Country, with movement

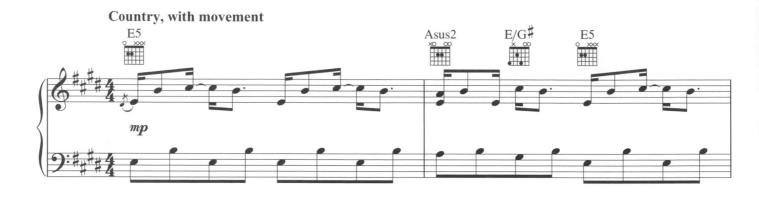

And

if I had a boat ___ I'd go out on the o - cean ___ and

IF WE WERE VAMPIRES

Words and Music by
MICHAEL ISBELL

know-ing that ___ this can't ___ go on ___ for - ev - er.

IN SPITE OF OURSELVES

Words and Music by
JOHN PRINE

Moderate Country Ballad

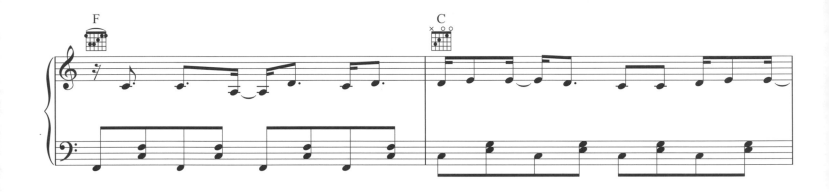

Male: She don't like her eggs___ all run-ny, she thinks cross-ing her legs___ is fun-ny.
Male: She thinks all my jokes___ are cor-ny, con-vict mov - ies___ make her hor-ny.

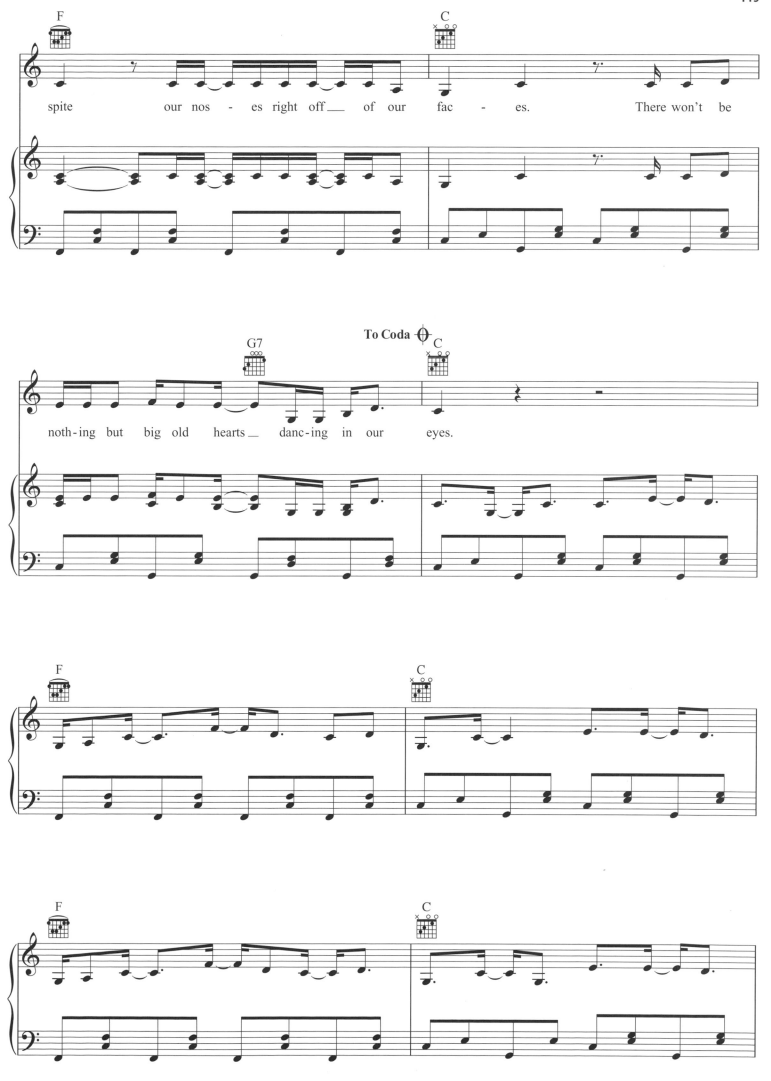

spite our nos - es right off ___ of our fac - es. There won't be

noth-ing but big old hearts ___ danc-ing in our eyes.

D.S. al Coda

CODA

eyes.   In spite of our - selves,   we'll end __ up   sit - ting on a

rain - bow. __   A - gainst all   odds,   hon - ey, we're the big __ door prize. __

We're gon - na spite our nos - es right off__ of our

fac - es. There won't be noth-ing but big old hearts__ danc-ing in our

eyes. There won't be noth-ing but big old hearts__ danc-ing in our

eyes.

Male (Spoken): In spite of ourselves.

slowing

IT AIN'T OVER YET

By RODNEY CROWELL

Moderately, in 2

Male 1: 1. It's like I'm sit - ting at___ a bus
2. rick - et - y___ old legs,___
3., 4. *(See additional lyrics)*

___ stop, and these wa - ter - ing for a train.___ Ex -
and these wa - ter - y eyes,___ it's

Additional Lyrics

3. For fools like me who were built for the chase,
   It takes the right kind of woman to help you put it all in place.
   It only happened once in my life, but man, you should have seen,
   Her hair two shades of foxtail red, her eyes some far-out sea blue-green.

4. I got caught up making a name for myself; you know what that's about.
   One day your ship comes rolling in, the next day it rolls right back out.
   And you can't take for granted none of this shit.
   The higher up you fly, boys, the harder it is you're gonna get hit.

HURRICANE

Words and Music by KEITH STEGALL,
STEWART HARRIS and THOM SCHUYLER

I don't mind the strain of a hur-ri-cane; they come a-round ev-'ry June.

The high black wa-ter, a dev-il's daugh-ter. She's hard,

she's cold and she's mean. But no-bod-y taught her it

takes a lot of wa-ter to wash a-way New Or-leans.

Solo ends

wash a-way New Or-leans. _____ Yeah! _____

Guitar solo - ad lib.

JACKPOT

Words and Music by
NIKKI LANE

Driving Country feel, in 2

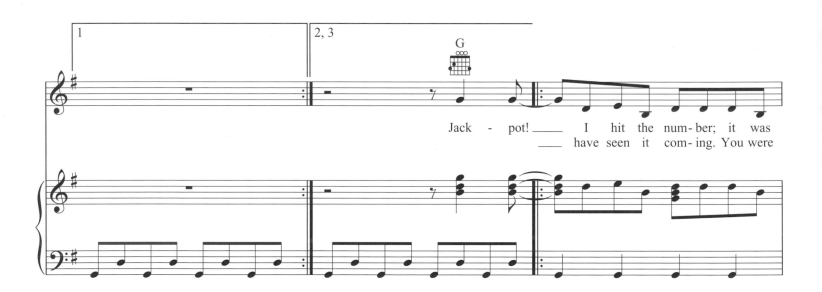

Jack - pot! ___ I hit the num - ber; it was
___ have seen it com - ing. You were

al - ways you. ___ I was look - ing for sev - ens, they were com - ing in ___ twos. ___ I was
al - ways there, _ stand - ing in the cor - ner with a warm, _ dark _ stare. ___ I had to

141

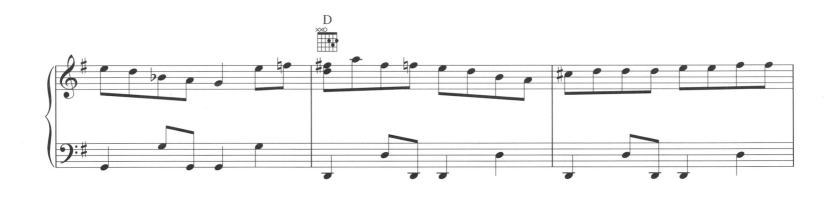

It's been a

long, long time since we placed our bets. ___ Cra - zy as it is, we ain't through

win - ning yet. ___ True love ___ don't come ___ 'til you lay it all down the line. ___

___ So, dar - ling, go all in ___ and give it

all you've got. ___ Put your quar - ter in the slot. It's gon - na be jack -

LET HIM FLY

Words and Music by
PATTY GRIFFIN

let him fly. ___

There's no mer - cy in a live ___ wire. No rest at

all in free - dom. ___ Of the choic - es we ___ are giv - en, ___

___ there's no choice ___ at all. ___ The

L.A. SONG

Words and Music by
BETH HART

LIVE AND DIE

Words and Music by SCOTT AVETT,
SETH AVETT and ROBERT CRAWFORD

All it will take ___ is just one ___ mo - ment, and _____
Left like a Pha - raoh, sing like a spar - row an - y - way, ___
Instrumental solo

* *Recorded a half step lower.*

Solo ends

And I wan-na love you and more._____

I wan-na find you and more._____ Where do you re-

Omit second time

side when you hide?___ How can I find___ you? 'Cause

I wan-na send you and more._____ I wan-na tempt you and more._____

LOST IN MY MIND

Words and Music by CHRIS ZASCHE,
JOSIAH JOHNSON, CHARITY ROSE THIELEN,
KENNY HENSLEY, TYLER WILLIAMS
and JONATHAN RUSSELL

Oh, my broth - er, ___ your wis - dom ___ is

old - er than me.

Oh, my broth - er, ___ don't you wor - ry 'bout

me. Don't you

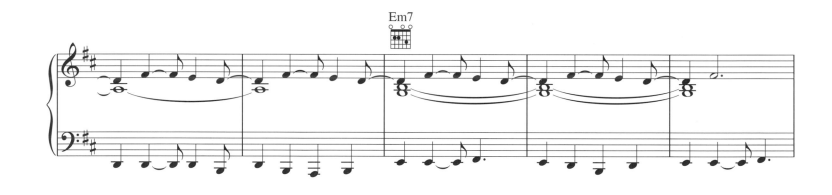

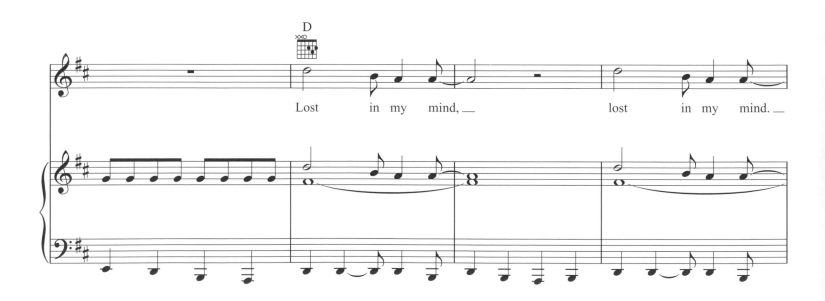

Lost in my mind, __ lost in my mind. __

Oh, I get _____ lost. _____

Oh, I get...

MANY A LONG AND LONESOME HIGHWAY

Words and Music by RODNEY CROWELL
and WILL JENNINGS

Easy Country feel, in 2

Yes, I had a wom-an love ___ me.
I be-lieve in love ___ and dan- ger,
My fa-ther, on his death ___ bed, told ___ me,

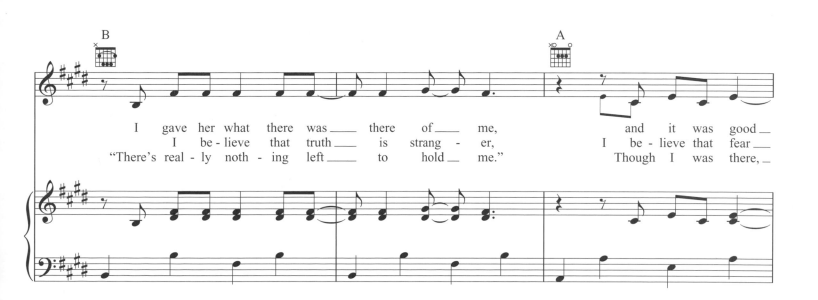

I gave her what there was ___ there of ___ me,
I be-lieve that truth ___ is strang- er,
"There's real-ly noth-ing left ___ to hold ___ me."

and it was good ___
I be-lieve that fear ___
Though I was there, ___

LOST IN THE LONESOME PINES

Words and Music by
JIM LAUDERDALE

Lost, lost in the lone- some __ pines, __ and __

nev - er more _____ I'll __ see.

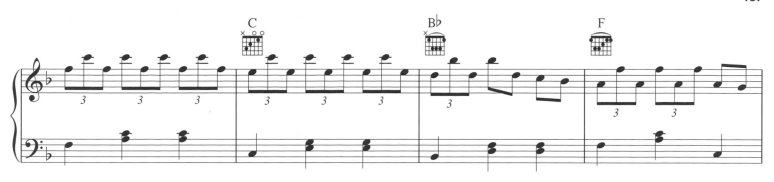

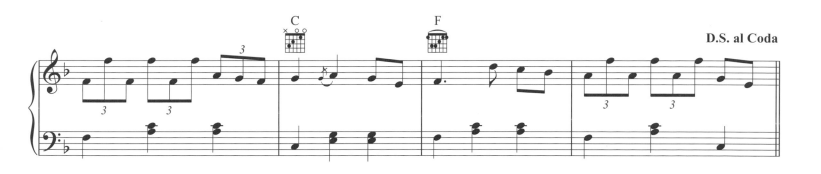

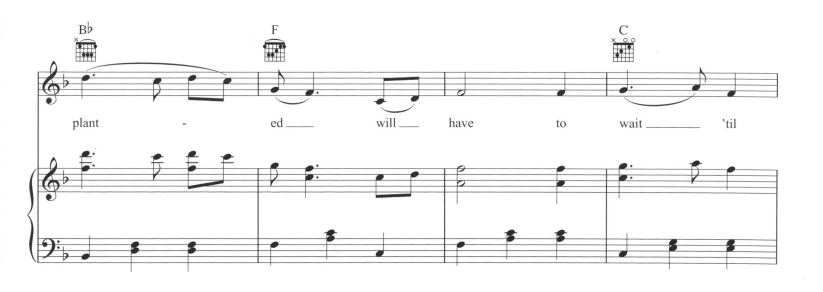

The ___ fields in rows not ___ plant - ed ___ will ___ have to wait _____ 'til

LOVE HAS COME FOR YOU

Words and Music by
STEPHEN MARTIN

She had a child by that man ___ from the bank. ___
But when she held that sweet boy ___ in her arms, ___

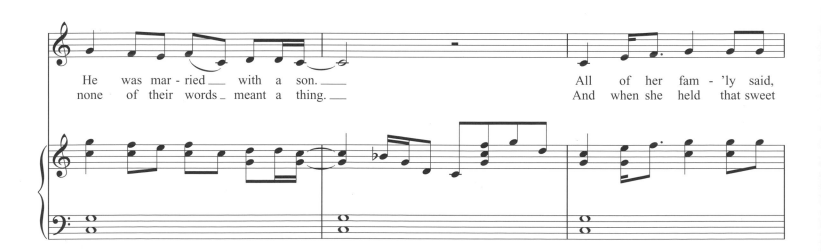

He was mar - ried ___ with a son. ___
none of their words ___ meant a thing. ___

All of her fam - 'ly said,
And when she held that sweet

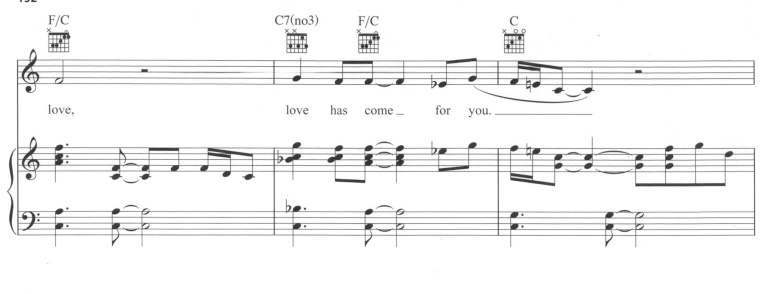

love,   love has come _ for you. _____

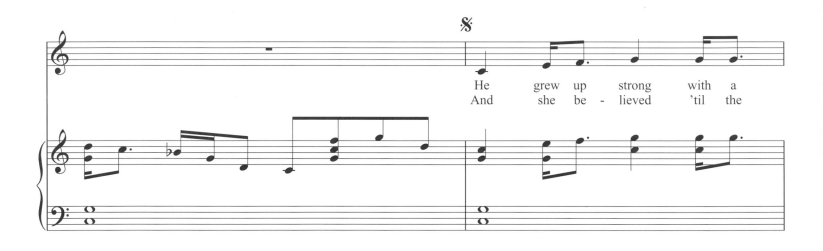

He grew up strong with a
And she be - lieved 'til the

heart ____ full of dreams, ____ and a good mind to make them come
day ____ that she died ____ he was giv - en from heav - en on ____

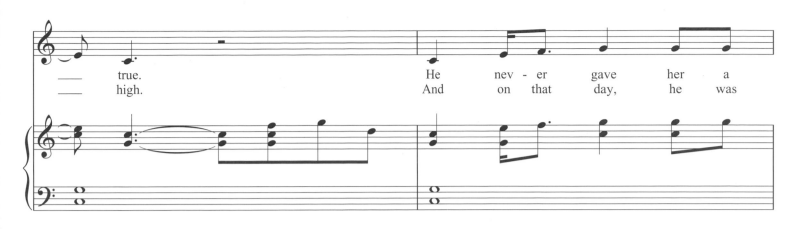

true.
high.

He nev-er gave her a
And on that day, he was

day's ___ worth of grief. _____ She lit up when he came ___ in-to the room. ___
right there by her side _____ when she heard the an-gels one more time. __

C

F/C

Love, love,

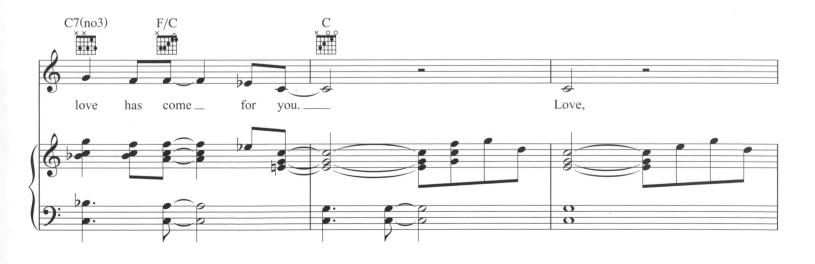

C7(no3)   F/C   C

love has come ___ for you. ___   Love,

love, love has come for you.

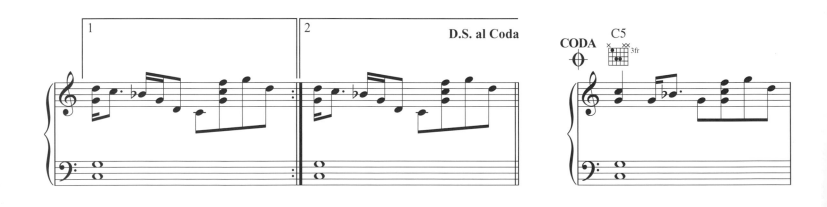

RETURN OF THE GRIEVOUS ANGEL

Words and Music by GRAM PARSONS
and THOMAS S. BROWN

MEMPHIS IN THE MEANTIME

Words and Music by
JOHN HIATT

I've got some-thin' to say, __
need a lit-tle shot of that rhy-
just get off __ of that

__ lit-tle girl, __ you might __ not like __ my style. __ But
-thm, __ ba-by, mixed up __ with these coun-try blues. __ I wan-na
beat, __ lit-tle girl, may-be we could find a groove. __ At

THE ROAD GOES ON FOREVER

Words and Music by
ROBERT EARL KEEN

Moderately fast, in 2

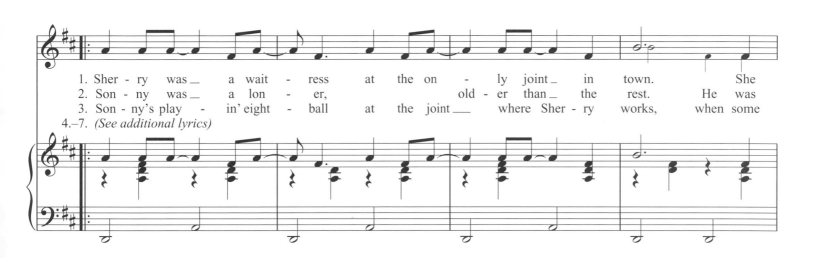

1. Sher-ry was __ a wait-ress at the on-ly joint __ in town. She
2. Son-ny was __ a lon-er, old-er than __ the rest. He was
3. Son-ny's play-in' eight-ball at the joint __ where Sher-ry works, when some
4.–7. *(See additional lyrics)*

had a rep-u-ta - tion as a girl who'd been a-round. __ Down
go-in' in __ the Na-vy but could-n't pass the test. __ So, he
drunk-en out - of-town-er put his hand up Sher-ry's skirt. __

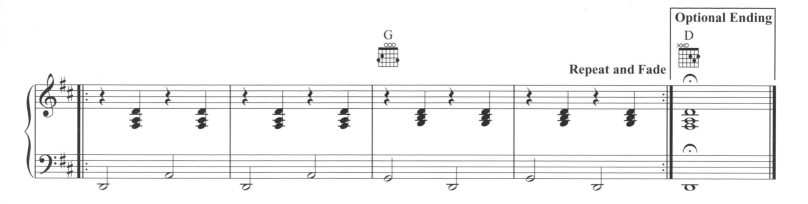

Additional Lyrics

4. They jumped into his pickup, Sonny jammed her down in gear.
   Sonny looked at Sherry, said, "Let's get on out of here."
   The stars were high above them, the moon was in the east.
   The sun was setting on them when they reached Miami Beach.
   They got a motel by the water and a quart of Bombay Gin.
   The road goes on forever and the party never ends.

5. They soon ran out of money, but Sonny knew a man
   Who knew some Cuban refugees that dealt in contraband.
   Sonny met the Cubans in a house just off the route,
   With a briefcase full of money and a pistol in his boot.
   The cards were on the table when the law came busting in.
   The road goes on forever and the party never ends.

6. The Cubans grabbed the goodies, Sonny grabbed the jack.
   He broke the bathroom window and climbed on out the back.
   Sherry drove the pickup through the alley on the side
   Where a lawman tackled Sonny and was reading him his rights.
   She stepped out in the alley with a single-shot four-ten.
   The road goes on forever and the party never ends.

7. They left the lawman lying, they made their getaway,
   Got back to the motel just before the break of day.
   Sonny gave her all the money and he blew a little kiss.
   "If they ask you how this happened, say I forced you into this."
   She watched him as the taillights disappeared around the bend.
   The road goes on forever and the party never ends.

MYKONOS

Words and Music by
ROBIN PECKNOLD

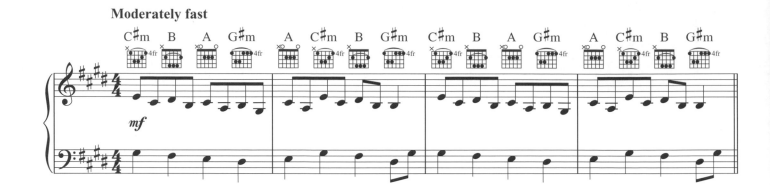

Whoa.

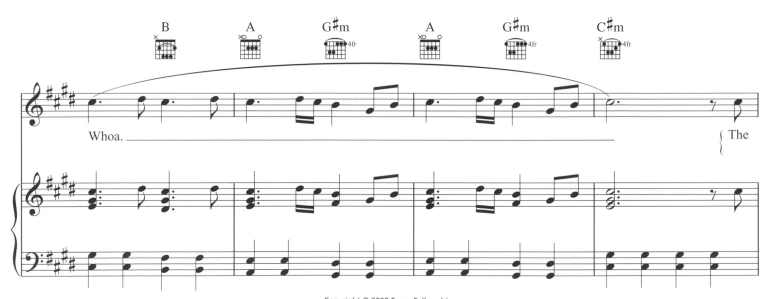

Whoa. _____ The

PANCHO AND LEFTY

Words and Music by
TOWNES VAN ZANDT

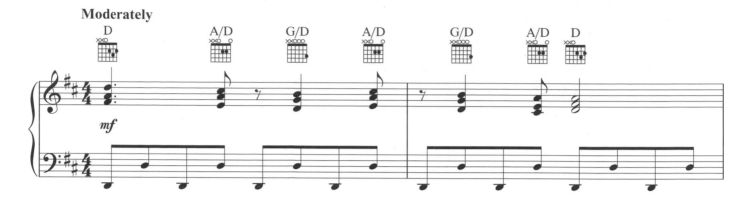

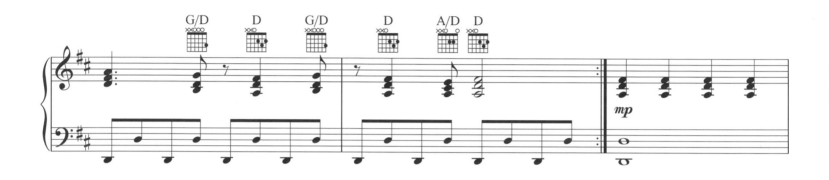

1. Liv-ing on the road, __ my friend, __ was gon-na keep you free __

2.–4. *(See additional lyrics)*

D.S. (3rd verse)
D.S.S. (Instr.)
D.S. (4th verse)
D.S.S. al Coda

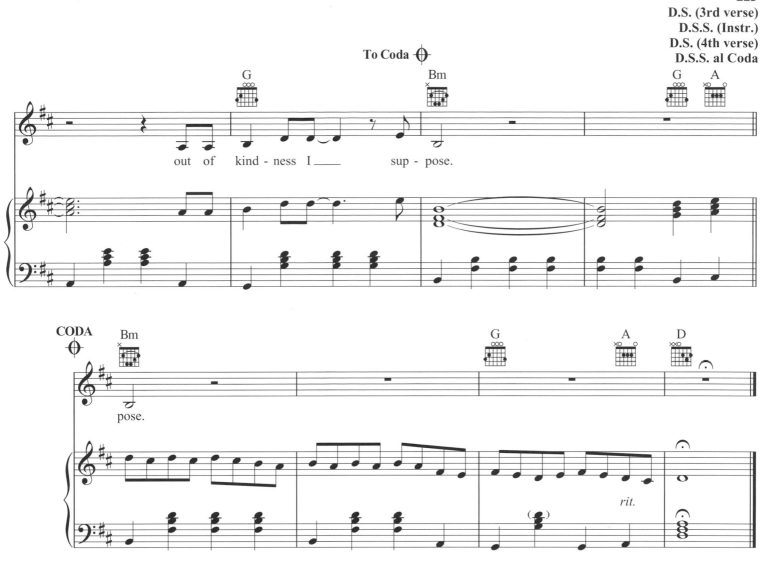

Additional Lyrics

2. Pancho was a bandit boy,
   His horse was fast as polished steel.
   He wore his gun outside his pants,
   For all the honest world to feel.
   Well, Pancho met his match, you know,
   On the deserts down in Mexico.
   Nobody heard his dying word,
   Ah, but that's the way it goes.

3. Lefty, he can't sing the blues
   All night long like he used to.
   The dust that Pancho bit down south,
   Ended up in Lefty's mouth.
   The day they laid poor Pancho low,
   Lefty split for Ohio.
   Where he got the bread to go,
   There ain't nobody know.

4. The poet's tell how Pancho felt,
   And Lefty's living in a cheap hotel;
   The desert's quiet, and Cleveland's cold,
   And so the story ends we're told.
   Pancho needs your prayers, it's true,
   And save a few for Lefty, too.
   He only did what he had to do,
   And now, he's growing old.

PINEOLA

Words and Music by
LUCINDA WILLIAMS

TEAR STAINED EYE

Words and Music by
JAY FARRAR

Moderate Country feel

1. Walk - ing down _____ Main Street, get - ting to
2. ___ trac - es of the
3. *(See additional lyrics)*

know the con - crete, look - ing for a _____ pur - pose _____
scars that came be - fore, hit - ting ___ the ___ pave - ment, ___

from a ne - on _____ sign. _____ I would meet ___
still ___ ask - ing _____ for more. _____ When the hours ___

Additional Lyrics

3. Like a man said, "Rode hard and put away wet."
   Throw away the bad news, and put it to rest.
   If learning is living, and the truth is a state of mind,
   You'll find it's better at the end of the line.

RED DIRT GIRL

Words and Music by
EMMY LOU HARRIS

Moderately, in 2

Me and my best friend Lil-li-an___ and her blue tick hound dog Gid - eon,

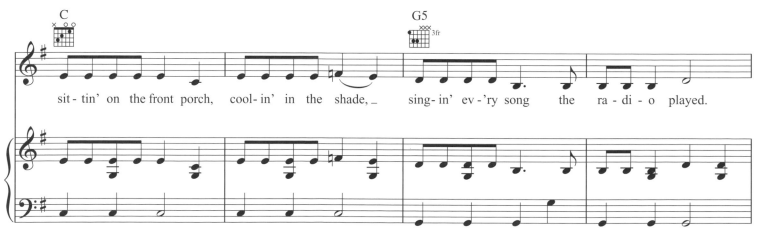

sit - tin' on the front porch, cool - in' in the shade, ___ sing - in' ev - 'ry song the ra - di - o played.

* Recorded a half step lower.

THE STORY

Words and Music by
PHIL HANSEROTH

Moderately

All of these lines ___ a-cross ___ my face ___ tell you the sto- -ry of who I am. ___ So man-y ___ sto- -ries of where I've been ___ and how I got ___ to where _ I am. ___ But these

Recorded a half step lower (Guitar Capo II).

Instrumental ends

TECUMSEH VALLEY

Words and Music by
TOWNES VAN ZANDT

1., 8. The name she gave ___ was Car-o-line, ___
2.–7. (See additional lyrics)

the daugh-ter ___ of ___ a min-er.

And her ways ___ were free, ___ and it seemed ___ to me ___

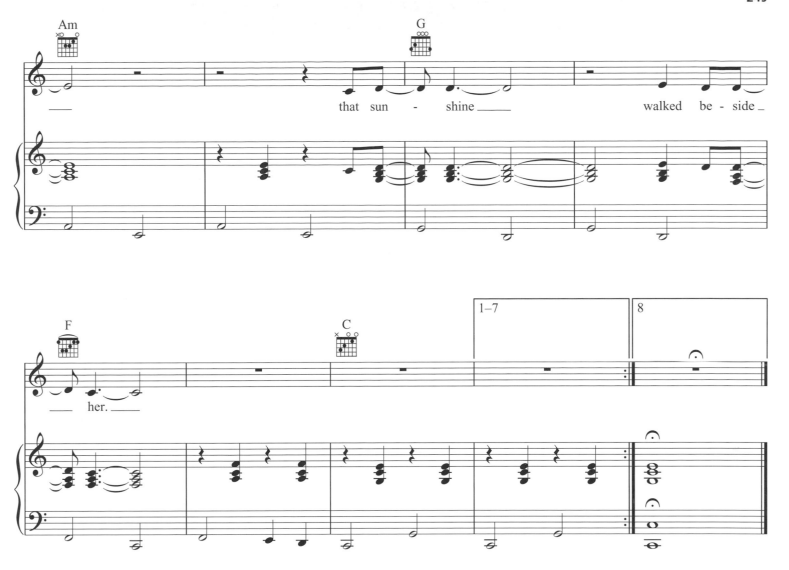

that sun - shine _____ walked be - side _____ her. _____

Additional Lyrics

2. She come from Spencer, 'cross the hill.
   She said her pa had sent her
   'Cause the coal was low, and soon the snow
   Would turn the skies to winter.

3. She said she'd come to look for work,
   She was not seeking favors.
   And for a dime a day and a place to stay,
   She'd turn those hands to labor.

4. But the times were hard, Lord,
   And the jobs were few all through Tecumseh Valley.
   But she asked around, and a job she found
   Tending bar at Gypsy Sally's.

5. She saved enough to get back home
   When the spring replaced the winter.
   But her dreams were denied; her pa had died.
   The word come down from Spencer.

6. So, she took to whoring out on the streets,
   With all the lust inside her.
   And it was many a man returned again
   To lay himself beside her.

7. They found her down beneath the stairs
   That led to Gypsy Sally's.
   And in her hand, when she died, was a note that cried,
   "Fare thee well, Tecumseh Valley."

THE TRAVELING KIND

Words and Music by RODNEY CROWELL,
EMMYLOU HARRIS and CORY CHISEL

Moderately, in 2

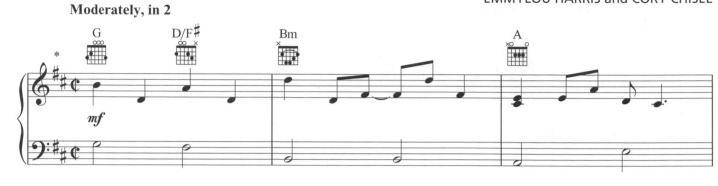

We don't all die young to save our
wind are young names to save our

spark from the rav - ag - es of
past. Some were rav friends of yours and

Recorded a half step lower.

TRAVELLER

Words and Music by
CHRIS STAPLETON

WAGON WHEEL

Words and Music by BOB DYLAN
and KETCH SECOR

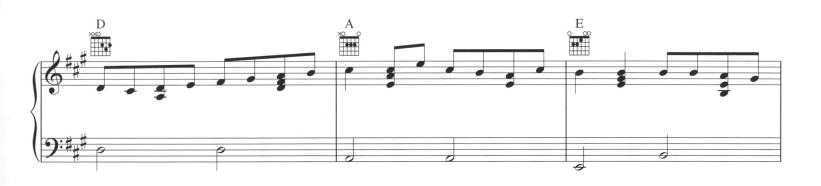

Head-in' down south to the
Run-nin' from the cold

wind and the rain. __ Rock __ me, ma - ma, like a south - bound train. Hey, __

ma - ma, rock __ me.

ma - ma, rock ___ me.

24 FRAMES

Words and Music by
MICHAEL ISBELL

Moderately

This is how you make your-self van-ish in-to noth-ing. And
This is how you see your-self float-ing on the ceil-ing. And

this is how you make your-self wor-thy of the love that she gave
this is how you help her when her heart ___ stops ___ beat-ing. What hap-

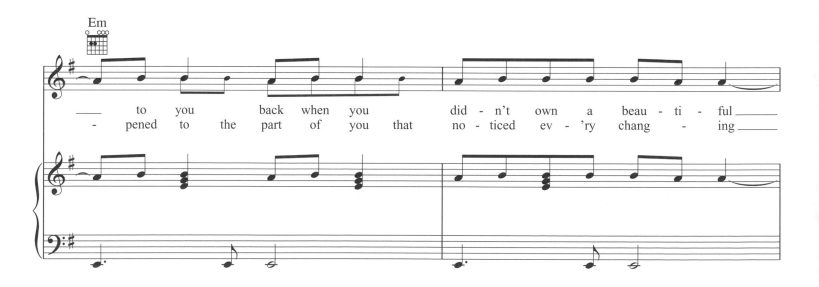

___ to you back when you did-n't own a beau-ti-ful ___
-pened to the part of you that no-ticed ev-'ry chang-ing ___

TWO MORE BOTTLES OF WINE

Words and Music by
DELBERT McCLINTON

WE CAN'T MAKE IT HERE

Words and Music by
JAMES McMURTRY

1. There's a Vi-et-nam vet with a card-board sign, sit-tin' there by the left __ turn line, a flag on his wheel-chair flap-pin' in the breeze, one leg mis-sin' and both __ hands free.

No one's pay-in' much mind to him; __ the V. A. bud-get's just stretched so thin. __ And there's
(2.) big ol' build-in' was a tex-tile mill __ that fed our kids __ and it paid our bills. __ But they

oh. _____ {5. There's a high-school girl with a bour-geois dream,
{8.–10. *(See additional lyrics)*

just like the pic-tures in the mag-a-zine _ she found _ on the floor of the laun-dro-mat. _ A

wom-an with kids _ can for-get all that. _ If she comes up preg-nant, what-'ll she do? _ For-

get the ca-reer, _ for-get a-bout school. Can she live on faith, live on hope?

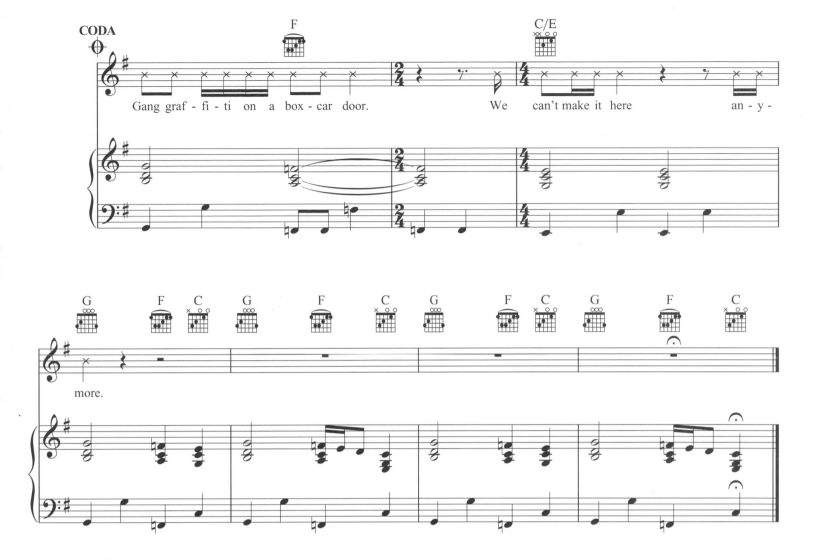

Additional Lyrics

8. Will work for food, will die for oil,
   Will kill for power and to us the spoils.
   The billionaires get to pay less tax,
   The working poor get to fall through the cracks.
   Let 'em eat jellybeans, let 'em eat cake.
   Let 'em eat shit, whatever it takes.
   They can join the Air Force or join the Corps
   If they can't make it here anymore.

9. And that's how it is, that's what we got,
   If the president wants to admit it or not.
   You can read it in the paper, read it on the wall,
   Hear it on the wind if you're listening at all.
   Get out of that limo, look us in the eye.
   Call us on the cell phone, tell us all why.

10. In Dayton, Ohio or Portland, Maine
    Or a cotton gin out on the great high plains
    That's done closed down along with the school
    And the hospital and the swimming pool.
    Dust devils dance in the noonday heat.
    There's rats in the alley and trash in the street.
    Gang graffiti on a boxcar door.
    We can't make it here anymore.

THE WEARY KIND
(Theme from CRAZY HEART)
from the Motion Picture CRAZY HEART

Words and Music by T BONE BURNETT
and RYAN BINGHAM

Moderately fast, in 2

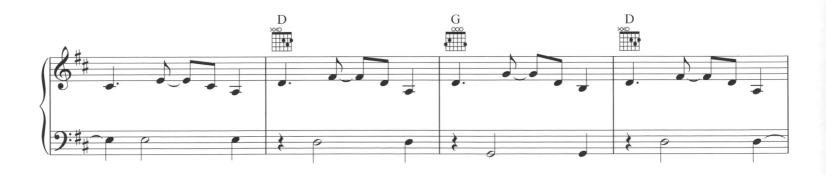

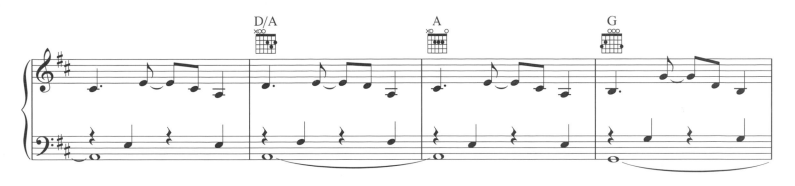

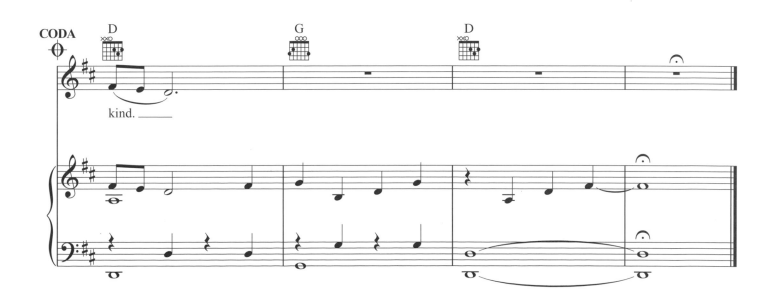

WINDFALL

Words and Music by
JAY FARRAR

Moderate Bluegrass feel

Now and then it keeps you ___ run - ning, ___ it nev - er seems ___ to die. ___ The trail's spent with fear, ___ not e - nough liv - ing on the out - side. ___

feet on the floor, two hands___ on the wheel,___ may the wind take your trou-bles a-

way.___

Tryin' to make it far___ e-nough___